Pelican

Poems

Mallory Nygard

Edited by Marie Trotter

First Edition

ISBN: 978 0 578 86907 0

for all those who have been hurt in
and by the Church,

may we find peace, healing,
and justice

Contents

He sins who
does not
become angry
when he has cause.

– St. John Chrysostom

Whoever causes one of these
little ones who believe in me
to sin,

it would be better for him to have
a great millstone
hung around his neck
and to be drowned
in the depths of the sea.

Matthew 18:6

Unsung

In the beginning there was a mother,
unnamed –
old now – herself almost a child
when one of her own
was taken in the beach house.

She read the sun-caught face
of her sweet, blond boy,
his always-gripping hands,
the unsung fear rising in his fidgeting fingers.
She couldn't unsee the damage done.

Unnamed mother,
unsupported, unbelieved, not
undaunted, she wrote what she read
in the hands of her son
to each father of the church.

In her own hand she broke the silence
that had broken her. Licked, pressed, sealed.
Her hand hovered over the maildrop, until
that sunburned future bishop appeared at the window.
She mailed the truth and trembled.

The Garden, Again

You betrayed me.

Stooped old man, the weight
of your own sin like stones stacked
on your shoulders until they are finally
enough
to drag you under.

Your words were honey and light,
but you were the hornet: killing
with a thousand relentlessly
repeated unseen stings

the hearts of women who only wanted to move
closer to something real.
Snake oil peddler.
Sweet-tongued charlatan.

Thoughtless man, reckless authority,
You preached humility while you held
your shrouded spear against the throat
of women who made pilgrimage to your feet
seeking
a tender and tended love.

Quieta non movere

Do not worry about him, they reassured.
Do not say anything, they cautioned.
Do not move him, they recommended.
Do not ordain, they decided.

Do not listen to her, they whispered.
Do not besmirch a good man's name, they admonished.
Do not see his hand slip up the boy's leg, they resolved.
Do not mention it, they repeated.

Do not say it again, they warned.
Do not listen to her, they dismissed.
Do not believe them, they wrote and wrote
until a mother tore the cold hand of silence from her lips.

Do not worry, he stamped the packet of papers.
He shut the filing cabinet. He locked the door.
I'm the archbishop, he said.
Nothing is going to happen.

Accusation

None of the deadly questions that hunt
me down, whisper in my ear, and indict me
are new under this rusted sun.

I have met all the conventional answers,
smiled cordially and shook their hands
in the beige conference hall of a cheap hotel.

Sharp corners and harsh truths
have been papered over into safe
platitudes and self-satisfied clichés.

Unable to answer my glare,
the naked brown man above
it all looks away, speechless.

The Song of Sarajevo

When Gavrilo shot the Archduke
as he rode unknowingly in his funeral motorcade,
the heir's blood a blooming poppy on his chest,
he surely did not anticipate
that the trigger pulled on the pale gray morning
would bring me to sit shaking
in my linen closet,
door closed and lights off,
wrapped in a worn comforter
trying to dredge my soul back into my bones,
one bitter February evening a hundred years later.

An unbroken line of broken fathers
was born from the bullet
fired that Sunday in June.
Including mine,
who dresses in midnight wool
under the blistering summer sun,
draped in clouds of tobacco
and discolored medals won
by boys led blindly into battle,
and reenacts his grandfather's war
every other Saturday
at the old fort, instead
of playing dress-up
with his lonely daughter,
alone in my brothers' world.

When he pulled the trigger
from under the green-striped awning
of Schiller's shop, did Gavrilo know
that the shot would echo
echo every day in the hearts of men
as they wrestled with their short-
sightedness and scar-crossed hands?

My father brought me back a bullet
once, when he returned from his war
games.
I set down a spade to receive the heavy
lead in my hands. He dropped it
in my palms and walked through the sandbox
without stopping.

I carry that bullet with me
through four moves,
never quite losing it
among the packing tape, the boxes,
the new faces and hours alone.

Billeted in a dorm built for students
as compensation for grinding down
the edges of their souls
on a war born from their fathers' unwillingness
to rebuild and repair, I learn
to cook for one. One plate, one fork, one
evening after another on my couch, alone.

That same scene replayed religiously
until I am – one late afternoon – invited
into a different darkened closet,
and sit knee-to-knee with a man
dressed in his all-black uniform,
a gold-lined slash of purple like a banner across his chest.
A man whose power I resent but cannot dismiss,
who by his chosenness
speaks his father's loving words
and holds his father's creation –
not self-destruction –
in his own hands
every day,
he asks me to release my clenched fist.

At his end, the damp and the rats
had made sure that even Gavrilo didn't
have a fist left to unclench.

On my way out the door
I dip my opening hand in the water
to be blessed, and with the softest ache,
the steel weight of my father's unhappiness
settles at the bottom of the basin
to wait and to rust.

Complicit

I tap my foot against
the cushioned kneeler
waiting
in line for my turn
to plead guilty.

Shifting, searching, unsettling,
I try not to stare at your stained men
preserved and perfectly posed,
casting shadows on my shoes
as I still fail
to surrender my dread.

For your sake
I have stood before
this unopened door,
curtained in velvet
and secret shame,
every Easter to try, but
every step on this ground hollows
me out until there is nothing
left to dry heave.

I shudder to know
that the indictment waiting
for me just beyond
the deep, red veil is the same

one waiting for your followers
who shuffled abusers
from St. Joe's to St. Pat's down the road and
from Our Lady of the Angels to St. Thomas the Apostle,
only one county over.

Forgive me, Father,
I rehearse, *for being like them.*
Any moment now, I will ask (on my knees) -
without deserving the gentle answer -
exactly what every man who laid
unwanted hands on the bodies of boys
given up to the altar would ask,
if they so dared:

To be unshackled once more, not just from the choosing
to do wrong,
but from the failure
to do good.

And our membership
in this same scarred body
makes me want to
scream
until the cry echoes off every paten
stained with the blood
of too-young martyrs.

I roll my shoulders and shake
the trepidation from my fingers,

aching to hold something breakable:
an abacus, a silver-stuffed clay bowl, a dove.
Pitched and smashed against sacred steps.
Yet again, I wonder,
Where is your fury?
There are tables here
for you to turn over.

I stand to go; too much,
the silence is too much.
But then the light overhead
turns from red to green.
The curtain opens.
An older woman,
taller than my grandmother,
but only just,
steps out.
A lifetime of carrying this membership
bends her small frame
toward the earth.
How much she has witnessed.
How much she has forgiven
in order to still love the weight.

Do you hear what we are saying?

The confessional is free.
The way is open.

One Bread, One Body

Pierced. Shattered.
Obliterated. Sacred no longer.
Can you feel it now?

With your insulated ears
(stuffed with pure white cotton,
fabricated, false)
and your eyes tightly shut
against the tortured little boy –
he's Mike's son –
sitting in the pew
next to you,
can you feel it thrust
into you so hard
you cannot breathe
through it?

Uncalloused hands
over your mouth,
on your chest,
down your legs

Can you feel it,
finally? Sliding
down your throat
until your screams
are silk-silent
and tongue-tied.

This scourge does not exempt
you. Can you feel
the unanswered tears
from the space where his tongue
should not have been?

So, please, put your money where
his mouth has been.
Spit the truth from between your lips
and lay your penance in their pockets.

Pelican

He opens his palm to me.
I crawl over and spread
my body on top of his.
I press my face into the well of his neck;
his fevered pulse, suffused with salt,
bathes my cracked lips.
My hands stretch to cover his
and his arms enfold me.

All those anointed hands
crucify us,
driving the spikes deeper,
penetrating our flesh
with relentless blows.

Lord forgive them, forgive me:
just a child, I did not know
what they were doing.

He pierces his chest,
and I bend down my head to drink
from his broken heart.

Go in Peace

The light above the stairs is burnt out
and another Sunday evening passes by
without my replacing it.

I climb into the darkness
again on my way to bed, leaving
my day on the landing.

When I wake at three
and see a moonbeam
nestling in the moss green blanket

tangled like a fetter around my feet,
I remember that I spent the whole weekend
contemplating the nature of

forgiveness.
I escaped the limestone cathedral
from the side door

and drove through my tears,
until I sat along the mantle's edge
of the river across from the still

dropping cliff, among the clover
where a lone black ant
crawled up the ridge of my shin.

Lying on my back in the shallow shadows,
I find that I now want to know more
than I did yesterday.

A List of My Sins (Found Scrawled on the Back of a Kroger Receipt)

Buying an extra side of cheese curds instead of tithing
Flipping off the asshole in the Jeep who didn't go
    through the yellow
Calling strangers assholes
Forgetting to turn off the air conditioning before leaving
    my apartment
Rolling my eyes at my mom when she can't see me
Rolling my eyes at my mom when she can see me
Pretending that the three pretzels I found on my front seat
    don't break the fast
Lying about brushing my teeth

I am on the brink
of casting off
all this banality
and running out to fall
in the most delectable,
creative ways.

Serving Song

I fill my table with a still sparking baklava,
a crème caramel so smooth Mary
herself could not resist a spoonful,
a lemon cake bathed in a sweet
raspberry drizzle,
a hazelnut shortbread waiting
for the coffee to be poured,
a pear tart crowned with walnuts
each dipped in caramelized maple,
a soft donut floating on a cloud of spun sugar.

Maybe if I had been in charge of desserts
for the Last Supper, Judas would have stayed.

Hope

Hope has not been a virtue to me,
but rather a curse,
a relentless curse of the awareness
of what is
not
with that brutal "yet"
hanging in the air
like a twitching body
at the end of a rope.

Time, dressed in the luxurious florals
and furs of tomorrow,
has stalked, haunted,
and trampled
over the life I have lived
without any regard for feelings
or appearances.
My past – even my present –
is reduced to
nothing
compared to the power
of what might
still be.

There's no use running. Hiding is impossible,
and ignoring ill advised.
There is nothing left

but to turn my face to the blazing sun
and be taken in –
body and soul –
to be destroyed

and, yet –

Nothing Greater

The last boy I smiled at –
in the library as I watched him
walk outside for a smoke break,
leaving a half-eaten box of fries
I brought to share and a stack of prints
that left me breathless;
Caravaggio's Paul, Van Gogh's Postman, and
Hopper's Nighthawks kept me
company in his absence,
as he stood in the courtyard, collar
turned up against the cool spring evening,
cigarette smoke incensing his cheekbones –
gave up his life to God.
Far off in the Italian foothills
where the sunflowers reach high
and bow to the pull from the east,
he sinks his teeth
into Anselm's lines on the expanse
of the creator,
and I am lost in a suburb
making peanut butter toast
for three meals in a row.

Psalm 22

With the Living Tree's bark rough on his back
and the lovebirds dancing in the sky,
Adam cried out his fear:
he does not – no, he cannot
endure
perpetual unwholeness.

Born into this ripe world,
he ached for more.

The Breath whispers, in humility,
It is not good to be alone.

The tears on his lips
convince me that when I
perched last night on a rounded root
of the knotted oak
in the park
by the lake
and cried about being
alone,
it was actually
all along,
a life-long
prayer.

What My Dowry Would Consist of (If We Still Did That Sort of Thing)

A shelf of unread American classics and the perception
of being well-read
Seven cardigans I tried so hard to resist buying
Three scars on my arms, all from baking pies
A gallery wall fit for the Renaissance patron of the arts
I was born to be
A stained-glass window of a daffodil in the sun made
by my own hands
A chipmunk who visits every day on her way to the oak
three doors down
My grandmother's cookbook, unfiltered Camels still
pressed between the pages
At least three jars of ground cloves, but somehow not
a single jar of black pepper
All the lyrics to "American Pie" ready at any time
A full set of pots and pans, minus the skillet (not
a metaphor)
A thoughtfulness born of years spent searching for you
in every person I met

How St. Lucy Could Have Lost Her Eyes

He lies in bed next to me, close
like the monarch to his woven chrysalis.

"Why won't you look at me?"

I ask the crook of his nose in profile against a sun-soft-
ened curtain.

His eyes flicker, following the colors on the ceiling, his
lashes shimmer like dew.

He wields his gentleness like a scalpel to my chest.

"Because it hurts you to be seen,"

He turns his face to mine
and I ignite.

Sitting Against a Tree Along the Tennessee River

Almost asleep in the midst of sky-held-water,
I wait for the shyness of the sun
to break through my half-closed eyes
before I have to join, again,
the ever-crawling interstate.

What is the point
of having all this
freedom
if I have no one
to give it up for?

Leftover meatloaf in my backpack.
Twice-warmed-over coffee forgotten
on the roof of my car. Under a crooked branch's
unassuming oversight, I close my eyes
to another day's promise
of emails and fluorescent lights.

What is more empty
than my mother's, my brother's
my priest's, repeated
assurances that
someday this
loneliness
will have been worth it?

Incarnation

The masseuse presses
her fingers into my thighs
where the doctor had held on
when he tried to stop the bleeding.

This is my body given up for you.

She smooths her fingers into my hips,
where the compounding, interlocking weight
of driving away from goodbyes said in fear
and shame slowly spread a delicate honeycomb.

This, given up.

She kneads the knots of my spine
where, preserved in the pillared salt,
I hide the burning self-contempt
born from neglecting my own brother.

This is for you.

She holds my shoulders
where, tangled among the stretched nerves and threaded
through the delicate veins along my clavicle, I hold
the unspoken story of my father's grease-stained hands.

Is this my body?

She pulls my arms long, finding the furrows of the veins
in my palms, pressing where He was pierced,
the man who offers himself – still – where I deserved
to die.

This is my body given up for you.

She troubles my temples,
catching a stray tear with her thumb,
trying to convince me of the giftedness
is being continually created.

This is you.

One Thousand Five Hundred and Seventy Miles

More times than I can count,
I packed up my car and left.

Crossing this country in the quest
for the romance of a small life far away
which is, actually, just
a blank slate at any cost.

Fooling myself that it is possible
to have a future
while I keep abandoning the past.

Standing still barely long enough
to admit I ache
for the courage to stay
somewhere long enough
to know
my own worth.

Maybe then I can finally
give this life away
to someone who will
use it well.

Endangered

My stomach is awash with the work of bees
who have claimed eminent domain
and daily dance a thunderstorm as I wait
for the long-promised honey.

Swallowtails roost in my lungs,
lonely kings over a barren expanse:
their accordioned wings reaching
for the song buried in the grave of my chest.

The soft-footed moss spiders shelter
behind my eyes; their lace-like silk stitches
the frayed ends of my nerves back together.
The sweet dreams are slowly coming back, too.

This flesh of mine has seen better days.
When those arthropods found
me curled on the floor, left for dead –
strip-mined for relics –

they whispered, *This is still salvageable.*
I invited them to cross the bridge of my tongue
and build a biome under my domed ribs that can –
if I have not yet spent all the mercy on offer –
sustain us all.

Like a lightning-hollowed oak, I am the core,
the enclosure, the fruit of their work.
I am reclaimed.
I don't have much to offer in return

(and even if I did,
how would they accept it,
these living jewels
who don't have hands to hold any gift?)

beyond my protection of the delicate balance
of tenderness in this ecosystem
of blood and bones and bugs.
So,

high collars and high waists,
layers of sweaters and sweatshirts.
I will wear everything to defend
these extinction-riddled creatures

that have made a home of me.
Never will anyone – any man –
take me from them
nor them from me.

An Elegy

It is unnerving
to be asked
to summarize
the whole of your life
in thirty seconds –

and disheartening
to attempt it.

Cannonization

In three hundred years,
when everyone who loved me
is forgotten,
a small man – bent with age
and responsibility – will read
my name out over an empty square.
"A patron saint for our times,"
he will intone, "for those who feel their hearts
twitch in their chests like frayed wire;
for those walking through their bare
apartments looking for their glasses;
for those who rest in the quiet
after hanging up the phone;
for those who sit in the sun
where at least their shadows are with them;
for those who pray out loud since there is no one
who can hear."

Sun Tea

Every summer when the sun turns
my skin the warm gold of a wilting
chrysanthemum, I remember
walking home from school and noting
the shape of each kind of leaf –
haloed by the afternoon gleam –
that waved from the trees lining
my neighborhood's streets.
I hadn't yet learned to keep my eyes
on the ground.

Not until the afternoon in late July –
before I met the stranger
in the mirror
of the high school bathroom –
when I skinned my knee riding my cousin's bike
and blood wound
like barbed wire
down my calf.

My aunt held me –
her left arm bent away
from her chest, a pointed reminder
of the accident she had on the way home
from her high school graduation –
as I cried and my knee stiffened.
I felt so old then.

When my mother picked me up that evening,
after she had spent the day's sunrays
sitting beside her brewing sun tea,
I limped to the car
and she did not ask me why.

Untethered

I have loved you – mostly from afar –
without reluctance
or restraint.
I only see you
for ten minutes
two times
a week.

When you look at me
through the waves and numbers,
a mere ghost on the screen,
I try to love
all my love for you
at once.

Imprisoned out here
(for now),
I cry for each breath
that falls away without
your eyes on mine.

If I was sent even farther
away, away to the moon
or Mars or the outermost edge
of the Milky Way, I'd still strain
my neck to see
the way you are a lily
blossoming
in the soft summer sun.

My only escape is the thought
that one day,
some day,
when this space will be gone day,
your little hand –
grown up and
wild,
patterned with the lines of your
sweet life –
will reach for mine.
Impossible to possess,
but nonetheless,
somehow,
still real.

Unfinished

I have not been able to write
the poem I dreamt,
the one about the time we buried
my grandfather in the dirt.

We buried him on a clear day in December.
In the days before backhoes, families kept the dead
on ice, waiting for the ground to thaw.
The departed could not cross a frozen Lethe.

Now we have mastered the earth with machines
and we dispatch our dead immediately –
out of sight and out of mind –
or burn them and avoid the decay altogether.

I helped carry my grandpa from the church to the hearse,
from the hearse to the deep, brown dirt
and across weathered white snow,
the wind unkind on my face.

The box was light.
He had broken free from his broken heart
and left behind only the piece
of him that had knelt to hold a frog to my cheek for a kiss.

The Third Week in July

For the last three days
a sunbeam has visited me
like an angel.

I know her by her fruits:
the ripened peaches
and soft plums
that burst like the bravest tulip in spring.

Dancing me around the room
on a breath,
away from the sharp
corner of the coffee table,

whispering about bumble bees
and chipmunks while nestled in my ear;

this is the knowing
I am not quite alone.

Poems I Will Never Write Having Not Been Offered the Job in Santa Fe

A Lament

Finally, Room to Breathe Again

Three Broken Pots and a Forgotten Cactus

Coming to Finally Love Cacti, or The Reconciliation of
My Deepest-Seated Childhood Fear

Is This the Old World or Am I Just a Modernist?

From the Plains to the Desert to the Grave

His Blood Pools in the Peaks, Not the Valleys

A Radioactive Sun Still Rises

The Sun This Close is a New Kind of Burn

The Ballad of the Archbishop (Dead but not Forgotten)

Shadowing Willa as She Stands in the Cathedral Deeply

Moved, Pen Already in Hand

The Road to Hell is Ice and I Am Finally Thawing Out

Lord, please, send me just for the poetry.

Hagiography

For the last three days
a sunbeam has visited me
like an angel.

I know her by her fruits:
the ripened peaches
and soft plums
that burst like the bravest tulip in spring.

Dancing me around the room
on a breath,
away from the sharp
corner of the coffee table,

whispering about bumble bees
and chipmunks while nestled in my ear;

this is the knowing
I am not quite alone.

Abandonment

Even Thomas knew his Summa
was not enough
to answer the sharp scrape of sin
echoing in the cavern of my chest
keeping me up
every Friday night for a year.

With the next and the next and the next
story of women and children –
and men –
thrust down on their knees
by unholy power,
the smoke from a straw-burning fire
drowns me a little more and a little more.

Over and again and still once more, I lift
my eyes to the naked
man and watch his unmovements
through the flames

just long enough to doubt –
to suspect that this scarcity is all
that will ever respond.

Could this be – is this really all –
this just might be the surrender –
no,

the abandonment
I have been so afraid of.

Thomas and Me Make Three

I know how Christ deals with doubters:
he drags you closer,
and plunges your hand in
his side until your fingers grip
his bloodied rib.

“Doubt this.”

Maybe I only doubt so much
as a means of being pulled in
to be consummated with the closeness
I dream of each morning
before the light.

For Judas, Who Hanged Himself

When the certainly-not-last-but-merely-the-latest report
breaks,
I cannot handle anything less than confrontation.
I drive to the chapel to stand accusingly
before the man, hanging high, who asked
everything of me and my childhood.

Moonlight breathes through the stained glass,
Unshared sorrows haunt the empty pews.
A white habit lightly sweeps the shadows
to the pace of steady prayers,
meeting the shaded silence where it lies
curled around the feet of winged stone spirits.
The friar clutches his black-roped beads in the growing
darkness as under his tired feet, the earth shivers.

I stop this priest,
a lost child before her father,
hesitantly holding out palms
cradling my somehow-still-gasping
lungs slowly draining
the sour deep red of life,
slippery in my hands like fish.
I try not to panic.
He tries not to recoil
from my touch.

How? and *Why?* rise with the last sputtering breaths
of the pale candle I had lit last Tuesday.

"When Jesus called the twelve," he whispers,
head bowed,
"he included a betrayer."

Trembling fingers wrapped around
the silver burning in his pocket,
Judas chose the tree that didn't give him
anything more than an end to his own agony.

Empty now after offering every piece –
I reach out, red-handed, into the shadows,
asking instead for ragged holes
on my hands and feet and side.
Surely, they will hurt less
than being slowly drawn
and quartered by the ceaseless
release of these damning glimpses
into a house built
of paper
pretending to be glass, safe
and transparent.

As long as I live, I will have
to bleed. I stuff a creased dollar –
the one with a corner ripped
off – into the offering box.
More blood money.

I strike a match against the rough edge
of the kneeler. I light
the wick of a new white candle.
Resigned to holiness for the men
who fucked
my church, I shove the burning wood
into the sand and pray
to the Lord,

goddamn it,
hear my prayer.

The Woman at the Well

She strides along the river,
under the persimmons on fire
and the dogwoods withering,
to the sun-soaked fountain,
and she shrouds her face in the water
until her eyes and ears and
thoughts and lips coated in bitterness
are washed clean
of the cabal who carry
the responsibility of a lonely son's
dying love.

Twilight afternoons,
weeklong sunsets,
years of daily dyings,
and still,
still no one –
not even one –
man –
vested, robed, or collared –
has knelt down beside her
to be refracted in the light.

Holy Grail

He holds his holy hands
out in front of himself,
showing me the frayed palms.
Silently he sings
the fullness
of his pain.

I cannot respond
except
to thirst,
yearning to catch the pooling blood
in the cup of my hands
and carry it to my lips.

I wonder if someday
it will not feel
like a martyrdom
just to have this –
just to have a
body.

Incensed

Before I pulled together a second notebook
from the remnants of my life –
the scraps saved from jean pockets in the laundry basket,
the pages of a half-read Robert Penn Warren novel,
and a handwritten birthday card from my grandmother
delivered more than a year after her funeral –

I burned my first notebook of poems
to convince myself that the words between
myself and God were enough.

The smoke drank in that irreversible risk,
and I heard my grandmother's voice –
"You can't lose what wasn't yours."

In the spray of sparks, I wonder
why I try
when every poem I want
has already been written.

Like a child, I remind myself
on each page –
Why doesn't the knowing last? –
that I write not to be special,
but to be human –
to be this human –
whose love, by some mystery,

speaks in the language
of lines, light, lilacs
to an audience of parched flames.

Thanksgiving, 1993

The first sunrise of my life I do not remember,
but my mother, every year,
tells of the way the world came up for air
after a day of blustering, blinding white winds.

In the midst of the worst snowstorm of a lifetime
(certainly my lifetime),
I woke. The glow of the cold sun
seeped thin and bare from behind sheer steel clouds.

I came to be not under the brilliant sunrise that carries
    painters to canvases,
nor the soft luminescence which pulls photographers
    from bar stools,
but the soundless gleam that calls the coyote to hunt
    until she is satisfied.

Almost a Love Sonnet

I want to be reckless with my love:
to give and to give and give and give.
But I am not mine to break in half.
If this is love, I do not want it.

I can no longer ask to wait
and see. In the monthly fall, my body
begs me to face my fear that time's
demands are impending, cruel, and impatient.

While I before had played too safely,
time has been calling me with wild-
ness wetting his lips, and he pulls me
to dance with his spirit one more time.

His generous gift is not exactly
what I expected: love enough.

The Long-Dormant Middle School Runner Within Me is Awakened

The lord of Emmaus
has already walked this road.

It has been so long since I last ran
(my shin splints, my flat feet)

I find my legs – free at last
of the weight of the water –

chasing the horizon
where his hem meets the earth.

Preservation

I pressed the azaleas between the pages
of a book on ancient Egyptian burial practices.
Mummified petals pulled wide by gravity
and rendered fragile by inattention.

Pressure and time make diamonds and oil,
but, add in my touch, and the blooming bushes
that wave from where the sidewalk ends
become light as lacewings.

The signs of spring I had broken off a branch
left an outline of mauve on the tomb picture;
ghosts of a day when I felt alive and killed
something growing to preserve that memory.

I cannot hold what I care about in these hands.
Fragile, the intake nurse stamps my file. Better to be left
in the care of others than to take care of myself. Better
to be taken care of than to fall apart at the slightest touch.

The scent of a still-smoldering summer sunset
on the prairie of my childhood – cottonwoods
consumed in the rich golden hour –
seeps from the maze of my lungs like a sieve.

Carried on that scent is the memory of running through
dry grass
under the widest blue sky towards my father's
outstretched arms after the cactus pierced my sole.
I ran like a daughter and – for once –
he was actually there.

This time, with help, I may let that remembrance rise
like incense from my expanding chest. I may finally let go
of the pressure, the weight, the time,
and learn how to handle myself with care.

A Prayer to St. Christopher

I am assured
this is the glade I will
wade through in order to be human
again.

And you know there is dry land on the other side?

Well, no.
There is a promise
of rest, and I am hoping
to one day believe
in the promise.

Then how do you cross?

For today, there is the sky above
and a lark
perched on my shoulder,
singing
me
on

Invitations

It is not lost on me
that while my priest reads the gospel
about Martha and Mary
I can't put my pencil down
and my poem away.

"Give it a rest," he invites me.
But I cannot.

You will wait forever,
but these lightning-bug-lines
breathe only for a moment
before they leave me forever.

I have need of these distractions,
and you have need of me.

So, you'll have to leave your seat
and chase after them with me.

Blessed are they
who hunger and thirst
for righteousness,
they will be satisfied.

Matthew 5:6

Author's Note

For the better part of the last three years, I have been contemplating the fact that the whole of my sacramental life in the Church has taken place in the shadow of the clerical sex abuse crisis.

I received my First Communion only three months after The Boston Globe released the first of their reports on the abuse and systemic cover-up in the Archdiocese of Boston, breaking open the seal that had silenced survivors of clerical sex abuse for decades.

That summer, the priest of my childhood parish – the priest who had said my First Communion Mass – was assigned to a new parish. Weeks later, he resigned in disgrace and was removed from ministry after admitting to sexually abusing multiple boys.

I was a child in his community, adults in my parish were aware of his pattern of abuse, and my parents knew that I looked up to and even loved him. I once declared to my mother during his going-away party in the school gym, "I'm never going to love the new priest as much as I love him." Despite all of this, no adult with any authority in my life ever said anything to me about that priest and what he did while in our midst, neither during his tenure nor afterwards.

The priest was – finally – dismissed from the clerical state by Pope Francis on February 8, 2021, almost 20 years after he admitted to the abuse.

Now, as an adult, the mass complicity in that silence haunts me.

I do not understand why some people and not others are hurt so badly within the Church, a community purportedly given to them as an example of love.

I do not understand why there were boys in my parish whose lives were unraveled by abuse and mine was not.

I do not understand a God who doles out a grace that seems so selective. Nor do I do understand a God who let himself fully experience on the cross the pain of his creation.

For so long, the broken and wounded of the Church were pushed into the shadows. Silenced. The men who were called to lead chose to protect the reputations of the powerful over the lives, the souls of the vulnerable.

I do not understand their choices, but most of all, I do not understand why no one is talking about this.

I do not understand why bishops and priests in dioceses across the country are still more concerned with avoiding liability, dodging payouts, and suppressing records than they are with their fellow members of the body of Christ who come to them speaking painful truths.

Is it too much to ask to listen? These truths were hidden for too long. No more.

"You will know the truth, and the truth will set you free," even if it is harrowing, explicit, and excruciating to bear.

As more people within the Church raise their voices in chorus for justice, I offer this collection of poems.

While not all of these poems were written in direct response to the sex abuse crisis in the Church, they were all born out of my wrestling with faith, membership, sin (my own and those of others in my life), expectation, freedom, and culpability.

In these pages, I have tried to tell the truth, to speak what should have been spoken from the beginning.

The proceeds from this collection will be donated to the Survivors Network of those Abused by Priests. SNAP offers support and resources to men and women who have been hurt by the Church.

Find more information and donate to support their necessary work at https://www.snapnetwork.org/.

Scripture to Pray With

Writing these poems has been a kind of prayer for me. At its most elemental, prayer is reaching out to the One whose arms are always – in each moment – already outstretched toward us. Prayer is the response and the return, the question and the silence, the wonder and the waiting, the insisting and the openness.

If you feel any of those inclinations after reading these poems – if you are changed – I invite you to come further in.

I have chosen a line or paragraph from Scripture for each poem in this collection, and I propose that you pray with the poem and the verse together. The Scriptures are overflowing with evidence that longing, angry outbursts, protests against injustice, and laments for sinners and saints alike are prayers heard by the source of all love.

As you pray with these words, contemplate the ways in which we allow injustice and hurt to continue unabated in our own communities. Contemplate the specific and particular ways God is inviting you to bring his truth, justice, and merciful love into the relationships and realities of your daily life.

God is vast enough to hold all our disappointment and disbelief. Our anger will never be more powerful than the fullness of God's justice.

Unsung
Matthew 21:21-22

The Garden, Again
Exodus 3:7-12

Quieta non movere
John 8:23-36

Accusation
Psalms 44:12-14, 16, 24-27

The Song of Sarajevo
Matthew 1:1-17
2 Samuel 11:1-27

Complicit
James 2:14-22

One Bread, One Body
1 Corinthians 10:15-17, 21

Pelican
John 19:14-18

Go in Peace
Psalms 23:2-3, 6

A List of My Sins (Found Scrawled on the Back of a Kroger Receipt)
Philippians 4:6-9

Serving Song
Luke 22:7-13

Hope
Genesis 3:1-11

Nothing Greater
Genesis 1:1-4

Psalm 22
Psalms 22:2-3

What My Dowry Would Consist of (If We Still Did That Sort of Thing)
John 6:60-69

How St. Lucy Could Have Lost Her Eyes
John 20-11-18

Sitting Against a Tree Along the Tennessee River
Genesis 2:16-18

Incarnation
2 Corinthians 5:6-8

One Thousand Five Hundred and Seventy Miles
1 Samuel 3:4-7

Endangered
the Exsultet sung during the Easter Vigil liturgy

An Elegy
Matthew 5:4

Canonization
Psalms 90:2-6

Sun Tea
2 Maccabees 7:20-23

Untethered
Matthew 1:18-24

Unfinished
John 11:1-44

The Third Week in July
1 Kings 19:11-12

Poems I Will Never Write Having Not Been Offered the Job in Santa Fe
Luke 7:1-10

Hagiography
Mark 5: 22-23, 35-43

Abandonment
Psalms 13:2-5

Thomas and Me Make Three
John 20:24-29

For Judas, Who Hanged Himself
Matthew 27:3-10

The Woman at the Well
John 4:4-30

Holy Grail
John 19-28-30, 33-35

Incensed
Exodus 3:1-6

Thanksgiving, 1993
Luke 1:26-38

Almost a Love Sonnet
Luke 7:37-50

The Long-Dormant Middle School Runner Within Me is Awakened
Luke 24:13-35

Preservation
Matthew 8:1-4

A Prayer to St. Christopher
Hebrews 11:1-3

Invitations
Luke 10:38-42

The collection as a whole
Isaiah 63:17-18; 64:4-6, 11

Acknowledgements

While so many of the topics and themes of this collection felt impossible to ever fully talk about, it is here at the end, at the point of gratitude that I find myself unable to communicate the depth of what I want to say. The support and encouragement I received while working on these poems seems too great to be caught by the limited words I have at my fingertips.
But, of course, I have to try.

Marie Trotter is one of the best readers I have ever had the good fortune to know and the best readers make the best editors.

Megan Ulrich shared her poetry, dinners, and friendship with me, and this collection feels like a paltry offering in return for the way she welcomed me into her life.

Stuart and Teresa Nygard read these poems with an openness that still makes me catch my breath.

Vance and Wesley Nygard's acceptance of these poems helped me know I am loved.

My early readers – Jessica Jacques, Alejandra Rohde, Alexandra Lengyel, and Carley Ubaldini – encouraged me to see that there was something worth working on in these words.

Taryn Okuma, Dan Gibbons, Gregory Baker, Kevin Rulo, and all the faculty of the English department at The Catholic University of America who taught me how to read well, write toward truth, and love the outcome.

"Canonization" and "A Prayer to St. Christopher" were originally published in Ever Eden Literary Journal.

"An Elegy" was written in memory of Tom Scalfaro.

"The Song of Saravejo" placed first in the poetry category and was named Best in Show at the 2021 Rehumanize International Create|Encounter.

About the Author

Mallory Nygard lives and writes in East Tennessee. Her poetry has been published in Ever Eden Literary Journal and and her poem "The Song of Saravejo" was named Best in Show at the 2021 Rehumanize International Create|Encounter. This is her first collection of poetry.

While wrestling in her attempts to understand who God is in her life, Mallory is a librarian at a Catholic elementary and middle school where she invites young people to develop a relationship with the written word. She hopes this lays a foundation for them to know – throughout their lives – the Word that still becomes flesh.

About the Cover Artist

Lauren O'Neill Curry is an artist and former Catholic youth minister from Baton Rouge, LA and now lives in Chattanooga, TN with her husband, dog, and cat. Her best days begin with the daily mass readings, a cup of coffee, and watching the sunrise before launching into a day of making art.

She approaches most art projects as a prayer of thanksgiving to God for giving her a gift she gets to use every day in countless ways.

More information about her art, design work, housewares, and illustrations is available on her website: www.laurenoneillartanddesign.com.

www.ingramcontent.com/pod-product-compliance
Ingram Content Group UK Ltd.
Pitfield, Milton Keynes, MK11 3LW, UK
UKHW020415250726
13967UKWH00007B/2647